Mo'
Letters
to Young
Black
Men

Mo' Letters to Young Black Men

More Advice and Encouragement for a Difficult Journey

Daniel Whyte III

MO' LETTERS TO YOUNG BLACK MEN

Cover Design by Bill Hopper of Hopper Graphics

TORCH LEGACY PUBLICATIONS: DALLAS, TEXAS;
ATLANTA, GEORGIA; BROOKLYN, NEW YORK

First Printing, 2008

The Bible quotations in this volume are from the King James Version of the Bible.

The name TORCH LEGACY PUBLICATIONS and its logo are registered as a trademark in the U.S. patent office.

ISBN-10: 0-9763487-7-2
ISBN-13: 978-0-9763487-7-1

Printed in the U.S.A.

This book is lovingly dedicated to

my Dad,

Daniel White Jr.

My brothers:

Anthony Martin & Mark A. White

My sons:

Daniel IV, Duran & Danyel Ezekiel

My daughters:

Daniella, Danita, Danielle, Danae`, Daniqua
and Danyelle Elizabeth,

who I hope will find good young black men, if that is God's
will for their lives,

And to,

All young black men across America and
around the world.

MO' LETTERS TO YOUNG BLACK MEN

TABLE OF CONTENTS

ON YOUR LIFE AND VITAL RELATIONSHIPS

ON YOUR LIFE AND RACE

ON YOUR LIFE AND THIS AND THAT

ACKNOWLEDGEMENTS

I wish to, first and foremost, thank God for putting within my heart a desire to do such a work as this, and for granting me the grace to get it done.

Second, I wish to thank my wife, Meriqua, for typing the manuscript, and also for editing and proofreading the manuscript. Thank you also to my two older children: Daniella and Daniel IV for formatting the pages, for helping with the proofreading, for taking care of other aspects of the ministry as I worked on this book, and also for being a great encouragement. I also wish to thank my younger children: Danita, Danae`, Daniqua, Danyel Ezekiel and Danyelle Elizabeth for doing great research on finding the quotes at the end of each letter, for helping in other aspects of the ministry as I worked on this book, and also for being a great encouragement.

A special thank you also to Bill Hopper of Hopper Graphics of Texas for, once again, doing a tremendous job on designing this beautiful cover.

Thank you to all of the readers of *Letters to Young Black Men* who took the time to write and let us know how much of a help and an encouragement that book was to them, and for expressing interest in this, its sequel, *Mo' Letters to Young Black Men*, thus serving also as an inspiration in the writing of this book.

May God bless each and every one of you.

PREFACE

I wrote *Letters to Young Black Men* out of two motivations:

First, the Lord impressed upon my heart to write this book because of the apparent great need among young black men in our community for Godly, loving, fatherly, advice and encouragement while on their journey in this life. I had a burden on my heart for my *"kinsmen according to the flesh."*

It disturbed me to see so many young black men messing up their lives so early in life, simply because they were not firmly guided in the right direction. So by the leading of the Lord, I decided to put pen to paper in hopes that God would use it to at least "save some."

I believe that the written word is still one of the most effective ways to reach people in a more concrete and permanent way. God could have written His Word in the sky, but He chose to record all His Words in a Book—the Bible. Note what author, Bud Gardner, said:

> *"When you speak your words echo only across the room*
> *or down the hall.*
> *But when you write, your words echo down the ages."*

The second reason why I wrote *Letters to Young Black Men* is because I am a child of the early sixties. What I mean by that is, I was born in the early sixties—arguably one of the most exciting periods of our American history. Indeed, in the words of Charles Dickens: "It was the best of times; it was the worst of times." For black people there could be no truer statement. Many agree that while we as a people were making major "strides toward freedom", freeing ourselves from the awful Jim Crow era and beginning to take our rightful place in American society, we began to lose some other important things, such as the good old fashioned way of raising our children, which included physical chastisement for doing wrong, and an emphasis on virtue and doing the right thing. In addition to that, when so many doors to employment opportunities began to swing open for our parents and grandparents, many naturally took on the mentality: "My children won't go through what I went through. They will have many of the things I did not have while I was growing up."

No one can blame them for that mentality. Coming out of what they came out of, anybody would have done the same. However, the results are still, none-the-less damaging, and because of that natural mentality, we have a generation of young people, who, for the most part: lack character, are materialistic, do not carry the values of their forefathers, and do not respect their parents, or anyone else for that matter. Our community has suffered many casualties and losses, and has planted seeds of destruction and pain that are immeasurable and that will probably take a generation to overcome.

These are the things that motivated me to write *Letters to Young Black Men* and now, *Mo' Letters to Young Black Men*. However, I did not write these books as an end in themselves.

I wrote these books for all young black men, but I wrote them primarily for the young black men who have faced some disadvantages in their young life, for I am convinced that the young life is the most important part of life. I wrote this book for the young black man who has no father, or who has a weak father; for the young black man who has no mother, or who has a mother whose priorities are out of order. I believe that if things are not done right in a person's childhood, it does not mean that he or she cannot cope with life when he or she gets older. However, there will be gaps in that person's life and those gaps will appear under pressure. These books are an attempt to help fill in some of those gaps in the lives of these young men.

As I said before, I didn't write these books as an end in themselves. I wrote these books to serve as a ramp which can get you on the right freeway—the freeway toward greater success and productivity in this life.

—Daniel Whyte III
Fort Worth, TX

MO' LETTERS TO YOUNG BLACK MEN

INTRODUCTION

I have been amazed at the overwhelming positive response to the national bestseller, *Letters to Young Black Men: Advice and Encouragement for a Difficult Journey*. I did not write the book to be popular, but I am pleased that it has been well received and still continues to sell nationwide. We give God the glory! I want to thank the multiplied thousands who bought the book, and the many who sent e-mails, letters, and made phone calls to tell us how much they appreciate *Letters to Young Black Men.*

It is my humble prayer that *Mo' Letters to Young Black Men: More Advice and Encouragement for a Difficult Journey* would be even more of a blessing and that it would be received with the same enthusiasm; but above all, that it would fill a great void in the lives of many young black men today.

Now, if for some reason you have received *Mo' Letters to Young Black Men* without having the benefit of reading *Letters to Young Black Men* first, may I encourage you to go to Amazon.com or to TorchLegacy.com and order a copy today. Or, you may just simply contact the person who gave you this copy. The reason why this is important is because this book, *Mo' Letters to Young Black Men*, is built on the foundation of *Letters to Young Black Men*. I would encourage you to read *Letters to Young Black Men* before this one, if you can.

Below are some of the important topics that I wrote about in

Letters to Young Black Men: Advice and Encouragement for a Difficult Journey:

1. The Main Thing
2. Get to Know Your Creator
3. The Awesome Value of Reading
4. The Marks of a Truly Educated Man
5. You Are Not Inferior
6. The Value of Working Hard and Smart
7. Women Folk!
8. Think For Yourself!

To ease you into **Mo' Letters to Young Black Men**, I am including the introduction to **Letters to Young Black Men** right after this introduction. Then, my first letter in this book is titled, "Connections". This letter will include some highlights of **Letters to Young Black Men**, with commentary, to help bring you up to speed. Right now, here is the introduction to **Letters to Young Black Men**.

—Daniel Whyte III
Fort Worth, TX

INTRODUCTION FROM
LETTERS TO YOUNG BLACK MEN: ADVICE AND ENCOURAGEMENT FOR A DIFFICULT JOURNEY

It appears that many people are concerned about the worsening conditions in the black community of America. And let's just be honest: we are in a bad way, generally speaking. I say, "generally speaking," because there are some blacks who are not doing badly at all. But the black community, in general, is not doing that well. You don't believe that? Just read the newspaper: we're killing one another, robbing our parents and grandparents, raping our women, selling death to the dying, going to jail wholesale, murdering our babies, not taking care of our responsibilities, and wiping out our future.

Why are we sinking in the sea of murder, drugs and mayhem? How can things be turned around? I believe that the problem lies largely with the black man, and I also believe that the solution lies with the black man. I am convinced that the key to turning black America around is to turn black men around. For any group of people to rise, their men must rise. And after they have risen, they must stay standing no matter what, and take their God-given position as the leaders of their families, churches, communities or what have you. These letters aim to help with that rising and standing.

These letters have been written in the midst of a very hectic schedule of traveling, editing an international publication, and working on several other publishing projects. These letters have also been written in the midst of being a black man, and a black husband and father, with all of the great and awful experiences that go with such an existence. I said that to say this: As I write these letters, I am not in some ivory tower somewhere philosophizing about life as a young black man. Rather, I am right in the middle of life as a young black man.

In short, these letters come from a sincere heart of a black man to the hearts of young black men.

Dear Y.B.M. (Please note that Y.B.M. will stand for "Young Black Man" throughout the book): I believe that this is a book that can absolutely revolutionize your life if you will let it.

See this book as a sign-post on the road of life, pointing you in the right direction. Read it, read it again, and then pass it on to another young black man struggling to find his way in this sometimes confusing and hostile world.

Daniel Whyte III
Tuskegee University Campus
Tuskegee, Alabama

PRAY!
THINK!
DO!

—Daniel Whyte III

SIR, I AM ASSUMING
THAT YOU ARE
ATTRACTED TO
WOMEN,
AND NOT TO MEN.

—Daniel Whyte III

YOU WANT TO LIVE
YOUR LIFE IN SUCH A
WAY THAT GOD CAN
TAKE YOU HOME AT
ANY TIME.
'LONGEVITY HAS ITS
PLACE.' BUT DOING
THE JOB THAT GOD
DESIGNED YOU
TO DO IS THE
ULTIMATE JOY.

—Daniel Whyte III

CONNECTIONS

Letter One

Dear Y.B.M.:

Well, it has been a while since I have written to you. I trust that you are growing spiritually, mentally, and otherwise in your life as a young black man.

Again, I want to thank you for the many kind letters and e-mails that I received from you in response to the book, *Letters to Young Black Men: Advice and Encouragement for a Difficult Journey*. It was good to hear from you.

As for me, my family and I are doing well. We have had a few challenges since I last wrote to you, but we are doing fine, thank the Lord.

As a courtesy to those who are reading these lines without the benefit of having read *Letters to Young Black Men*, I will hit some of the highlights to bring you up to speed. The book, *Letters to Young Black Men,* is divided into three major sections:

ON YOUR LIFE—SPIRITUAL

ON YOUR LIFE—EDUCATIONAL

ON YOUR LIFE—AS A YOUNG BLACK MAN

I started the **On Your Life—Spiritual** section, with the following statement:

Recently, I was speaking at a church in Orlando, Florida, and I saw a sign on the front of the pulpit, that read:

> *The Main Thing*
> *Is To Keep*
> *The Main Thing*
> *The Main Thing.*

From there I dealt with the following important subjects:

- The Main Thing
- Get to Know Your Creator
- How to Obtain the Blessings of God
- Your Road Map to Real and Lasting Success
- Tap Into Unlimited Power
- The Encouragement Place
- Pulling Others Out of the Fire

I started the **On Your Life—Educational** section with this statement from the letter entitled: "The Awesome Value of Reading":

First of all, may I kindly encourage you to spend as much time as you possibly can reading.

I dealt with the following subjects in that section:

- The Importance of Increasing Knowledge
- The Obstacles to Getting a Good Education

- Graduating From College and Still Ignorant and Unlearned
- The Marks of a Truly Educated Man
- With All Thy Getting, Get Wisdom and Understanding
- Please Learn "Yourself" a Little Etiquette

In the third and final section of the book, **On Your Life—As a Young Black Man**, I began with this statement:

Down through the years, I have noticed that one of the marks of a "Morehouse man" is confidence. And that is what I want to write to you about today.

From that section I went on to deal with the following subjects, with the one entitled "Women Folk!" being the most popular and the most controversial:

- You Are Not Inferior!
- Take the Road Less Traveled
- Take Full Responsibility
- Talk and Listen to Every Older Man Past Fifty That You Possibly Can
- Learn About Where You Come From
- The Value of Working Hard and Smart
- Things I Wish Someone Had Told Me When I Was Twelve
- How to be Really Cool
- Women Folk!
- Think For Yourself!

This little highlight section doesn't do the book justice, because every chapter in the book is of vital importance to your life as a young black man. When you find some time, go down to your local Barnes and Noble or go online to Amazon.com and order a copy of **Letters to Young Black Men: Advice and Encouragement for a Difficult Journey**.

Until then, I hope that this will help you get up to speed.

Pray! Think! Do!

Daniel

P.T. (Power Thoughts):

- Our faith must be sustained by our passion for dignity and our trust in God.
  —Adam Powell Jr.

- Lift up yourselves...take yourselves out of the mire and hitch your hopes to the stars.
  —Frederick Douglass

- There is in this world no such force as the force of a man determined to rise. The human soul cannot be permanently chained.
  —W.E.B. Dubois

OH! THE MISTAKES I'VE MADE

Letter Two

Dear Y.B.M.:

I hope my last letter helped you get caught up to where we are.

No one likes to admit to making mistakes. It is amazing what lengths we go to to try and cover up our mistakes and failures. Below are three reasons why it is a waste of time to try to cover up our mistakes and failures:

1. Covering up our sins and failures never causes us to prosper. Proverbs 28:13 says: *"He that covereth his sins shall not prosper: but whoso confesseth and forsaketh them shall have mercy."*

2. People who are not transparent rarely help other people.

3. Many already have your number—you just don't know that they do.

I remember while I was a student at Baptist University of America (BUA) in Decatur, Georgia, we had mandatory chapel services each morning at around 11:00. We had a different preacher each chapel hour. I enjoyed most of the preachers who preached, but there was one preacher by the name of Raymond Hancock who visited regularly, and whom the entire student body loved to hear. The difference between this preacher and the other preachers was like night and day. The reason: this preacher had the humility and ability to not only preach the Word of God, but to be transparent at the same time. It made all the difference. I learned through those chapel services that the great preachers and the preachers who help people the most are those who keep it real.

With that said, allow me to share with you some personal and painful mistakes that I made in my early years. My purpose in sharing these mistakes with you is so you would avoid them, because contrary to popular belief, some mistakes done in youth leave scars that can last a lifetime.

The first big mistake I made as a young man was **having sex before marriage**. I know that may sound punkish. Nevertheless, it was a big mistake. Like so many brothers, I took pride in my sexual "conquests" for a long time. But as time went on, what I was not proud of was the pain I caused so many people: the young lady I was involved with, the mothers and fathers, the grandparents, the aunts and uncles, the children born out of wedlock, and the child that was aborted when I was only fifteen years old, because the mother and I, in ignorance and immaturity, thought it was the best thing to do at that time. This murdering of an innocent life haunts me even after thirty years.

LESSON: I believe the real reason God forbids sex before marriage is because it hurts so many people for a long time—sometimes for a lifetime. Although sex is a lot of fun, it is far more a spiritual thing than a physical thing. Watch this! I say it is more of a spiritual thing because it is only through sex that God brings another spiritual being into the world to fellowship with Him.

The second big mistake I made was **not taking my early**

education seriously. I, like many of my school friends, had no idea how important our education was. In my mind, school was a place to tolerate, a place to skip, a place to run the girls, and a place to have fun. Oh, how I regret not taking my schooling seriously. Because I didn't, I had to play catch up when I got older. Son, that is exactly where the system messes up young black men. The system lets you into high school and because you have the wrong mentality when you enter high school, and because the teachers don't have the time nor the patience, they let you keep your playful, wrong mentality, and at the end of your high school days, they pass you on to graduate just to get rid of you—knowing that you haven't learned anything. If you waste your school days in high school, and still manage to graduate, it is very likely that you will not be able to handle college, because college work is built on high school work.

LESSON: You will have plenty of time to play after you get your Doctorate. For now, don't make the mistake I made of not taking school seriously. Learning is best done while your mind is young and while you can grasp things better. So, hit the books while there is still time.

The third big mistake that I made as a young man **was running with the wrong crowd**. The irony of this is, I was a preacher's son. Not only was I a preacher's son, but I had the same name as my dad, and on top of that, my dad was on television each Sunday morning with his Gospel program.

Being a preacher's kid, I know the reason why many preachers' kids are worse than the other kids. The preachers' children are trying to fit in with the in-crowd. My friend, Bill, and I were big time preachers' kids, yet we raised more hell, drank more liquor, and had more women than any of our other friends. We were the leaders of the pack. I remember one incident: some of the children on the school bus were joking with me about being a preacher's son, and I remember blurting out, in an attempt to fit in, that "I am going to drive the bus to hell." That is frightening. But I remember making that statement.

I remember on another occasion, one of my "girlfriends" and I were sitting on the front porch watching the sun go down. During the course of our conversation, she told me that I was going to be a preacher one day like my father. I don't know what came over me, but I cursed her and I swore that I would never be a preacher. Why? Because while I was sitting on that porch with her that evening, preaching was not on my mind at all. I despised anything to do with preachers. I wanted to fit in, and preachers' children normally do not fit in with the in-crowd.

LESSON: Stop trying to be like others and be yourself. If you think you need a crowd, get with the crowd that is going to church and the crowd that is getting A's in school. Lynn Swann said: "Why try to fit into a crowd that after you graduate from high school, you will probably never see again?"

As you will see in the next letter, I have made some more mistakes, but these are some of the big ones. Avoid these pitfalls, and you can save yourself a lot of heartache and trouble, and you can get down the success highway much faster.

Avoiding Mistakes,

Daniel

P.T.:

- All men make mistakes, but only wise men learn from their mistakes.

  —Winston Churchill

- A man's errors are his portals of discovery.

  —James Joyce

- When you make a mistake, don't look back at it long. Take the reason of the thing into your mind and then look forward. Mistakes are lessons of wisdom. The past cannot be changed. The future is yet in your power.

  —Hugh White

- Running with the wrong crowd will never help you.

  —Ryan Cabrera

OH! THE TROUBLES I'VE SEEN #1

Letter Three

Dear Y.B.M.:

> *"Man that is born of woman is of few days,*
> *and full of trouble."*
>
> —Job 14:1

Boy, Job got that right!

Jesus said: *"These things I have spoken unto you, that in me ye might have peace. In the world ye shall have tribulation: but be of good cheer; I have overcome the world."*

—John 16:33

Some years ago, I preached a sermon entitled: *Songs in the Night*. In that sermon, I brought up the idea of God-ordained troubles and self-imposed troubles. Well, I have had some of both, but I am going to mainly deal with self-imposed troubles. In other words, I am going to deal with the troubles I brought upon myself. YBM, remember this:

> *"Be not deceived; God is not mocked: for whatsoever a man soweth, that shall he also reap."*
>
> —Galatians 6:7

The main trouble I brought upon myself stemmed from my bad attitude as a teenager. When I got into my early teens, I developed a very bad attitude—particularly toward my dad. I knew how to play the hate dad/love mom game very well. I don't really know why I despised my dad so much during those days, other than the fact that he was a preacher. (But I will say this: if a father does not lead the family in the way he should, and if he does not spend quality time with his children, those children will probably grow up bitter toward him.)

Anyway, I had a really bad attitude toward my father—talking back, accusing him of abusing my mother, etc. Well, one day, I was in the bathroom with the door locked, doing my usual running off at the mouth, and talking back to my dad because he wouldn't let me have the car, or something. I thought I was safe with the door locked. Friend of mine, my dad got tired of my talking back, and he tore the door down and burst into the bathroom. I thought I was going to die that very hour. I thought I had seen the end of my days. Son, you can avoid a whole lot of trouble by maintaining a good and positive attitude.

Little did I know that my attitude would seep out and affect other areas of my life as well. While in high school, I carried that bad attitude on to my job with me, and even though I was the best worker on the job, my boss, Terry Buchman, got tired of putting up with my bad attitude and one day he told me never to return to the job again. That's right, I got fired from an after-school job. This took me by surprise seeing I was the best worker on my job at the time. This is when I learned the lesson that attitude is more important than performance. A few weeks later, I went back to Mr. Terry Buchman, and apologized for my attitude. I changed my attitude, and he gave me my job back.

Now, I know this may sound trite, but it is so true: "Your attitude determines your altitude"; your attitude determines how high you go in this life. If you have the right attitude towards your parents, you will go very high in this life. A bad attitude toward your parents and to others in authority, will bring you low.

"Honour thy father and thy mother: that thy days may be long upon the land which the Lord thy God giveth thee."
—Exodus 20:12

Ephesians 6:1-3 also tells us: *"Children, obey your parents in the Lord: for this is right. Honour thy father and mother; which is the first commandment with promise; That it may be well with thee, and thou mayest live long on the earth."*

I credit an old Bible-believing preacher by the name of Charles McKinney down in Biloxi, Mississippi, for helping me to get my attitude changed. He was really the first one who had the guts to consistently stand up against me and my bad attitude, and I thank God he did. I sign off...

With a New Attitude,

Daniel

P.T.:

- Troubles are often the tools by which God fashions us for better things.
  —Henry Ward Beecher

- If i were asked to give what I consider the single most useful bit of advice for all humanity it would be this: Expect trouble as an inevitable part of life and when it comes, hold your head high, look it squarely in the eye and say, 'I will be bigger than you. You cannot defeat me.'

—Ann Landers

■ The greatest discovery of any generation is that a human being can alter his life by altering his attitude.

—William James

■ Attitude is the way you mentally look at the world around you. It is how you view your environment and your future. It is the focus you develop toward life itself.

—Selected

■ The way out of trouble is never as simple as the way in.

—Edgar Watson Howe

OH! THE TROUBLES I'VE SEEN #2

Letter Four

Dear Y.B.M.:

The second trouble that I brought upon myself during my young years was loving women and using women for all the wrong reasons. Dear brother, when God made women, He made something! To me, there is nothing on God's green earth more beautiful than "Phat" women. Nothing! (For the ebonically challenged, "Phat" means very fine.)

I am an out and out Christian man; I am a minister of the Gospel of Jesus Christ; I pray and read the Bible every day; I've been married for twenty years now to my first and only wife, but I don't think I will ever get over God's handiwork of the second and third quarters of a woman's body. Most men, if they are honest, will tell you that their greatest struggle in life is the same struggle that David and Samson experienced—"Phat" women folk. We criticize Adam for casting all of humanity toward the gates of hell, but the fact of the matter is, if we had seen the first, second and third quarter of the naked body of Eve, not only would we have eaten the apple, we would have eaten the entire tree and then we would have helped to plant another one. You know I am right about that.

Be that as it may, the truth of the matter is, men who violate the Word of God by having sex with women they are not married to, will pay for doing so. Look at King David and Bathsheba— God took away the son who was born to them out of their sin, and trouble never left his house. Samson's lust for women caused him to get deceived by a conniving woman named Delilah, and he ended up with his eyes plucked out.

You may ask, why do I have to pay for having sex with a woman I am not married to? Notice what God says in His Holy Word on this matter.

"Flee fornication. Every sin that a man doeth is without the body; but he that committeth fornication sinneth against his own body."
—I Corinthians 6:18

"Now concerning the things whereof ye wrote unto me: It is good for a man not to touch a woman."
—I Corinthians 7:1

Suffice it to say, that every time, not just sometimes, but every time I had sex with a woman I was not married to—it was great while it lasted, but trouble and problems followed the pleasure. Millions can testify to the fact below:

"Stolen waters are sweet,
and bread eaten in secret is pleasant."
—Proverbs 9:17

Now, I have never been the romantic type. I am not naturally inclined to try to win a girl by buying her candy or flowers, or taking her out on expensive dates. But I have found other ways to win women over. Since I have never been the "sweet" type, I have never been hurt by a woman. In other words, I have never been "played" by a woman. Unlike Samson of old, I have never given my heart to a woman. I just don't roll like that. I have never considered any one girl my girlfriend even though she may have thought she was my girlfriend. In fact, I was seeing more than one girl at any given time when I was younger. That being the case, I have never held any bitterness or animosity toward women folk.

Like Samson, however, I "loved" women too much and all for the wrong reasons. The truth is, I didn't love women for who they were, but for what I could get from them. When I got what I wanted from them—which was sex—trouble always followed.

You ask what kind of trouble followed?

1. After a period of casual sex, the relationship would begin to sour. It begins to sour because even though she was giving me what I wanted, I had no intentions on giving her what she wanted, which was commitment, love, and affection.

2. If the young woman became pregnant, that created another set of problems, which are self-explanatory.

One problem came up that haunts me to this very day—and it has been over thirty years now since it happened. I was seeing this one girl for sex repeatedly. To be honest, we were having a lot of fun together—until she got pregnant. We were very young—about fifteen. We both decided that it would be best to get an abortion. Somehow, I came up with the money and she and I went down to the doctor's office and had the baby aborted. For some strange reason, the doctor wrapped the aborted baby in a napkin and gave it to her. Once we got in front of her house, we both looked at the aborted baby boy after which we placed him in the woods across the street from her home. Believe it or not, we both continued having sex and we did not stop until I got one of her best friends pregnant. Fortunately, for the child and for our own consciences, her best friend kept the baby.

Later in life, after I got saved, I learned that what that young woman and I did was murder an innocent child. Every now and then, I think about that baby buried in the woods across the street from her house, and the guilt and shame is painful.

The moral of that story, if you will is, when you break God's law, God's law has a tendency to break you.

Again, remember this verse!

"Be not deceived; God is not mocked: for whatsoever a man soweth, that shall he also reap."
—Galatians 6:7

3. Even if you actually have children out of wedlock and things do not work out between you and the baby's mother, as a father and as you get older, you suffer the pain and heartache of not having the privilege of loving and raising those children. Every now and then you will feel guilt and shame regarding that as well.

4. Baby Mama Drama

So, young black man, do not have sex outside of marriage because trouble is sure to come.

"But if ye will not do so, behold, ye have sinned against

*the Lord: **and be sure your sin will find you out.***"

—Numbers 32:23

Avoiding More Trouble,

Daniel

P.T.:

■ Failure is instructive. The person who really thinks learns quite as much from his failures as from his successes.

—John Dewey

■ Any sex outside of the marriage bond between a man and a woman is violating God's law.

—Jerry Falwell

■ When trouble calls on you, call on God.

—Selected

OH! THE TROUBLES I'VE SEEN #3

Letter Five

Dear Y.B.M.:

> *"One trouble with trouble is that*
> *it usually starts out like fun."*

I trust that you are doing well. I hope that you have made the decision not to make any of the life-altering mistakes that I have made and thus suffer the troubles that I have experienced.

I am sure I surprised and broke my mother's heart many times as a teenager, but there were two instances, in particular, when I really broke her heart. I have already told you about one situation and that was when the young woman and I made the awful mistake of aborting that baby. What I didn't tell you was that, for some strange reason, my mother went into my little gray safe that I kept under my bed in my bedroom, and she found the receipt from the doctor's office. She was livid. She was speechless. She was so hurt she could not even bring herself to punish me for what I had done. I knew then I had hurt her deeply.

Another time that I really hurt my mother (and this relates to the point of my running with the wrong crowd and not thinking for myself), was when my boys and I took my mother's car to go steal some beer, run some women, and party. Well, everything would have been fine if I had not run the car into the front of the store building in an attempt to get away from the store manager and the police. I guess I was so nervous I put the car into drive instead of reverse when we were trying to make our get-away.

I crashed into one of the pillars in the front of the building nearly bringing down one side of the canopy. Although we escaped and went on with the partying, in the back of my mind, I was figuring out how I was going to explain to my mother the huge dent in her new Granada. (Back then the Granada was the black man's Mercedes.)

Well, the gang and I came up with a plan: we would get a rubber hammer and beat the dent out while she was at work at the telephone company in New Bern, N.C. The fellows and I got together, decided to skip school that day, and we went to my mother's job, with the rubber hammer, where we started beating the dent out of the Granada. It was around 10:00 a.m., and it just so happened to be my mother's break-time. She was passing by the only window that was in the building when she saw us beating on her new Granada. I believe my mother was more hurt than angry. But she was enough of both to kill me if she could have gotten away with murder. My mother actually came to my bedroom that night and told me if I didn't straighten up I was going to a reformatory school. Her tone of voice left no doubt in my mind that she was very serious. I didn't know what a reformatory school was, but I knew I didn't want to go there.

This was just another instance when I should have avoided trying to be cool and run with the gang, but instead should have followed my own mind.

The lesson for you, young black man, is this:

1. Think for yourself and lead others in the right way. Never be a follower, and never condone or be an accomplice to wrongdoing. *"Enter ye in at the strait gate: for*

wide is the gate, and broad is the way, that leadeth to destruction, and many there be which go in thereat" (Matthew 7:13).

2. Don't think that running with the wrong crowd is cool. Remember, *"There is a way that seemeth right to a man; but the ends thereof are ways of death"* (Proverbs 14:12).

3. Honour your parents so much so that you won't do negative things that would cause them shame, embarrassment, heartache, and loss. *"My son, hear the instruction of thy father, and forsake not the law of thy mother"* (Proverbs 1:8).

I am telling you while you are young that: it is cool to stay in school and learn; it is cool to run with positive people who are learning and growing; and it is cool to think for yourself.

Yours for Avoiding Further Trouble,

Daniel

P.T.:

■ Don't think you're on the right road just because it's a well-beaten path.
—Author Unknown

■ Do not follow where the path may lead. Go, instead, where there is no path and leave a trail.
—Ralph Waldo Emerson

■ You have enemies? Good. That means you've stood up for something, sometime in your life.
　　　　　　　　　　　　　　　—Winston Churchill

OH! THE JOYS I'VE HAD

Letter Six

Dear Y.B.M.:

"Happiness depends on the happenings, but having joy does not depend on the circumstances. Joy comes from God and you better get some."

I pray that you are not in any trouble.

I apologize for staying on trouble so long, but sometimes trouble comes double.

In my previous letter, I shared some of my mistakes, failures and troubles in hopes that you will not make them. Now, I want to share with you how God delivered me from fleeting happiness to permanent joy. Then, I want to share with you the three greatest joys of my life.

Up until December 19, 1979, at the age of nineteen, my happiness was dependent on what was happening. You know what I am talking about. You have been there. When I was a little boy, if the sun was shining and the sky was blue, I was happy; but if the clouds covered the sun and the day was overcast, I was sad. When I was playing football, I was happy; when I was made to go to choir rehearsal, I was sad. When I could stay at home and watch the Dallas Cowboys play, I was happy; when I had to go to church, I was sad. As I grew a little older, when I was drinking and partying, I was happy; the next day, I was sad. That was how I lived my life up until December

19, 1979, because on that memorable day I accepted Jesus Christ as my personal Saviour.

Now, remember that I told you earlier how I used to hate preachers and churches. Well, on that night, December 19, 1979, a young man, by the name of Michael Lewis, came to my dorm room on Kessler Air Force Base around 8:00 p.m., and showed me from the Bible how to truly be saved from hell. Even though I had been in church all of my life, this was the first time anyone took the time to show me from the Bible how to be saved from hell. I accepted Jesus Christ that night and God completely filled my life with joy—"A joy the world can't take away." I am telling you the truth. That joy has never left me since I accepted Christ as my Saviour. Every day has been and is a sunshiny day, as far as I am concerned. It is truly a "*joy unspeakable.*" The Lord will do the same thing for you as well. There is nothing like having God's joy. It will beat happiness every time.

Since that time, God has added joy to joy. My three greatest joys in life are:

1. Knowing the Lord as Saviour, and my relationship with Him through prayer and through His eternal Word.

2. My family. There is no other place on God's green earth where I would rather be than home with my family. I really mean that.

3. My third greatest joy in life is doing something that matters beyond my life span. Jesus gave me a purpose to live for, and that purpose is to serve Him with all my heart, mind, soul, and body. By the grace of God, by the time

I was thirty-three, I had traveled around the world preaching the Gospel. I had also written several books and edited a Christian magazine.

It is my prayer that you will be a man who has the same joy in your life as I have in mine.

With "joy unspeakable",

Daniel

P.T.:

■   This is the true joy in life, the being used for a purpose recognized by yourself as a mighty one.
—George Bernard Shaw

■   Joy does not simply happen to us. We have to choose joy and keep choosing it every day.
—Henry Nouwen

■   Joy is not in things; it is in us.
—Richard Wagner

WOMEN FOLK! #2

Letter Seven

Dear Y.B.M.:

I trust that you have God's joy.

In this letter, I want to shift gears a little and add some good points to a letter I wrote to you in **Letters to Young Black Men.** It is the letter that I entitled "Women Folk!" Now, to my surprise, mothers, fathers, and men loved this letter, but many young wives and young women did not care for it that much. However, they handled it better than I expected. Well, this letter will be just as controversial, but at the same time just as helpful. The responses will probably be the same across the board. With that said, here are some more things that you need to know regarding the women folk.

What should you expect from a good woman based upon the Word of God?

1. **She should be a help to you and not a hindrance.** If she is tearing down everything that you are building up, she is not worth having. *"And the Lord God said, It is not good that the man should be alone; I will make him an help meet for him"* (Genesis 2:18). *"Every wise woman buildeth her house: but the foolish plucketh it down with her hands"* (Proverbs 14:1).

2. **She ought to be trustworthy.** If you can't trust your

woman, she is not worth having. *"The heart of her husband doth safely trust in her, so that he shall have no need of spoil"* (Proverbs 31:11).

3. **She should be industrious and a good keeper at home.** A lazy woman will not be of any benefit to you. *"She seeketh wool and flax and worketh willingly with her hands"* (Proverbs 31:13). *"She looketh well to the ways of her household, and eateth not the bread of idleness"* (Proverbs 31:27).

4. **She ought to be eager to satisfy you sexually.** *"The wife hath not power of her own body, but the husband: and likewise also her husband hath not power of his own body, but the wife. Defraud ye not one the other, except it be with consent for a time, that ye may give yourselves to fasting and prayer; and come together again, that Satan tempt you not for your incontinence"* (I Corinthians 7:4-5). Young brother, you should not have to beg, plead, and jump through hoops in order to have sex with your wife. She should do this enthusiastically.

5. **She should voluntarily submit her will to yours** without smirking, blowing, or rolling her eyes. *"Wives, submit yourselves unto your own husbands as unto the Lord, for the husband is the head of the wife even as Christ is the head of the church: and he is the Saviour of the body"* (Ephesians 5:22-23).

6. **If you have to hit her, you don't need her!** I repeat: if you have to hit her, you don't need her! If you have to

hit her, you don't need her!

7. **If she cannot boil water before you marry her then do not marry her.** She should know how to cook.

8. **She should love you.** *"That they may teach the young women to be sober, to love their husbands, to love their children"* (Titus 2:4).

9. **She should respect you.** *"Nevertheless let every one of you in particular so love his wife even as himself; and the wife see that she reverence her husband"* (Ephesians 5:33).

10. **She should carry herself in a Godly manner.** *"To be discreet, chaste, keepers at home, good, obedient to their own husband, that the word of God be not blasphemed"* (Titus 2:5).

After preaching in a church in Germany, and while eating dinner with the pastor and his wife at their home after the service, here's what this dear pastor's wife told us at the dinner table:

Daniel, let me tell you something about women—it is the nature of women to want the control and reigns of the relationship. Now she will not know what to do with the reigns of the relationship, but she wants them. Deep down in her heart of hearts, she wants you to take the lead, but she will never let you know that. If she gets the reigns of the relationship she will not give them up without a fierce fight. You must be a man and take the reigns from the get go and keep them, and you will have less trouble in your marriage.

If any of the ten things mentioned above are not happening, she is violating the Word of God and making you and your children miserable.

By the way, contrary to popular thought in the black community, if *you,* the head of the household aren't happy, nobody should be happy. Whether you want to be or not, you are the king of your castle—reclaim your throne. In case you are worried, your dear woman will never be happy in this life until she is making you happy and comfortable. God wired women to get their pleasure from pleasing their husbands and caring for their children. If you have a woman who does not understand that, you don't need her.

Below are some other truths that may or may not be backed by Scriptures, but all truth is God's truth and I think I have the Spirit of God in me:

A. Just as you are sizing her up to see if she is going to be a good wife for you, she is sizing you up to see if you are going to be man enough to handle her. If she detects that you are not man enough to handle her, then you won't be the one she marries.

B. I want to say again: love her, have a great time with her, talk with her, have fun with her, but keep the reigns of the relationship firmly in your hands.

C. "It takes a real man to be married to a black woman."
—Olin Wiley

D. The biggest mistake my dad ever made was letting my mother run the show. Son, don't make the mistake of letting your wife run the show. You set the pace.

E. Many men, today, are hen-pecked, controlled, and dominated by their wives.

F. It is the strangest thing—your woman wants you to lead. She may kick, buck and fight against your leadership, but she wants you to lead.

G There is not a good woman on God's green earth who does not, deep down, want you...

- To keep her in check
- To hold her accountable
- To be jealous over her
- To protect her from messing up her life

H. You might err sometimes, brother, but you will be better off being firm in your leadership of your wife than lax. Women have a tendency to feel insecure when the man is lax and not paying attention.

I. Women want love and affection from a real man.

J. Deep down, a good woman does not want a carbon copy of herself.

K. Yes, your woman would like for you to seek her advice on some things, but believe it or not, deep down she wants to know that when the chips are down she is with a man who can think and operate independently of her.

L. Sometimes good sex can solve some problems that talking cannot.

Dealing with the Women Folk well,

Daniel

P.T.:

■ A virtuous woman is a crown to her husband: but she that maketh ashamed is as rottenness in his bones. —Proverbs 12:4

■ Behind every great man, there's a great little woman who helps make him that way, his helpmeet.

—Unknown

■ For the lips of a strange woman drop as an honeycomb, and her mouth is smoother than oil: But her end is bitter as wormwood, sharp as a twoedged sword.

—Proverbs 5:3-4

■ The husband is really the boss when it comes to the natural family, and God's Word clearly says that women should obey their husbands.

—Selected

■ A wife is someone cherished in a very
special way,
Who puts the joy in living with her
sweetness day by day.
A wife is someone close enough to really
understand,
To inspire and to encourage and to lend a
helping hand.
A wife is one who makes a home a happy
place for all.
Who shows her special thoughtfulness in
ways both big and small.
A wife is someone wonderful who always
has a smile,
Who keeps her husband happy and
makes his life worthwhile.

—Selected

ON YOUR LIFE AND VITAL RELATIONSHIPS

ON YOUR RELATIONSHIP WITH YOUR WIFE OR WIFE TO BE

Letter Eight

Dear Y.B.M.:

May I encourage you to get married. Contrary to what many think, marriage can and should be a joy and a pleasure, not a pain and a burden. Do not judge marriage based on what you have seen of other people's marriages—even your parents or grandparents. Marriage can be and should be fun, and if you do it the right way, that is, God's way, it will be fun. Before I mention to you some points on how to have a happy and prosperous marriage, let me share some things with you on why you ought to get married.

First, you ought to get married because in this life it is good to have someone special to help you and encourage you along the way. A good wife can be that special someone and thus can become your best friend. Ecclesiastes 4:9-10 states: *"Two are better than one; because they have a good reward for their labour. For if they fall, the one will lift up his fellow: but woe to him that is alone when he falleth; for he hath not another to help him up."*

Second, you ought to get married to avoid the sin of fornication, which is sex before marriage. Don't let anyone fool you, whenever you sin, you hurt others indeed, but you hurt yourself more. Sin is a bad thing! "Sin blinds, sin grinds, sin binds", and don't you forget that. First Corinthians 6:18 tells us to: *"Flee fornication. Every sin that a man doeth is without* *the body; but he that committeth fornication sinneth against his own body."*

Third, you ought to get married so that you can be a husband and guide to a young black sister. Notice I said "young black sister". Now, I am not a racist by any stretch of the imagination. I have white people in my family. I love them just as much as I love my other family members. We also have white people working in our organization, and we all get along quite well.

Now, dear brother, you have a right to marry who ever you wish, but may I strongly encourage you to marry a good black woman for these reasons:

  a. You will help your race
  b. You will eliminate the added pressure that comes with being in a mixed marriage.

Contrary to what others may be telling you, or what you may have heard others say, you can find a good black woman if you pray one in.

Fourth, you ought to marry to have children that you can raise up to serve the Lord in this present age.

Fifth, society in general, looks askance at a young man past the age of twenty-five who does not have a girlfriend or some woman on his arms, or who shows no signs of getting married, or no interest in marriage. People begin to wonder: Is he gay? Does he have homosexual tendencies?

With that said, here are six important things that you must do to insure a happy marriage:

1. *Pray, and under the Lord's leading, take the time to choose a good woman to be your wife.* A bad woman can and will make your life miserable.

2. *Refuse the notion that marriage must become a drudgery.*

3. *Make the choice to love your wife.* Your wife will not look her best all of the time; love her anyway. She may not feel her best all of the time; love her anyway. She may not say the best things all of the time; make the choice to love her anyway. Believe it or not, love is a choice and not a feeling.

4. *Avoid bitterness.* Do not allow yourself to live a life of bitterness. Bitterness and strife will only make you, your wife, and your children miserable, and your marriage will probably end in divorce because of it. We are told in Ephesians 4:26, 27 and 31: ***"Be ye angry, and sin not: let not the sun go down upon your wrath: Neither give place to the devil." "Let all bitterness, and wrath, and anger, and clamour, and evil speaking, be put away from you, with all malice."*** It's quite all right to show some anger in order to let your wife know that you are serious about some things—just do not sin in the process.

5. *Be the head of your family.* Do not buy into the modern philosophy of making the woman the head, or giving her the same authority as the husband. Listen, friend, God wants you to be the head of your family. If you are a man at all, in your heart of hearts you want to be the head of your family. Believe it or

not, your wife, in her heart of hearts, wants you to be the head of the family, and even your children want you to be the head. So, be the leader of your family. Have confidence in the God that leads you and in yourself, and have confidence that the decisions you make under God's leadership are right for your family and for others.

Dear brother, one of the biggest reasons why the African-American community is in the shape that it is in today, is because women run the home and much of everything else. Don't be a part of continuing this negative side of our heritage.

6. *Seek God's guidance each day.* Pray this prayer daily: "Lord, lead me, guide me and direct me through this day in all I and my family do. Help me to make wise decisions."

Your marriage can be a great blessing to you if you have the courage enough to follow God's leadership and be the head of your household.

For strong black husbands,

Daniel

P.T.:

■   When a man marries a woman, they become one—the trouble comes when they decide which one.

—Selected

■ Hen-pecked husbands soon learn that he who hesitates is bossed.

—Selected

■ Nothing makes a marriage rust like distrust.

—Unknown

ON YOUR RELATIONSHIP WITH YOUR FATHER

Letter Nine

Dear Y.B.M.:

> *"Children's children are the crown of old men; and the glory of children are their fathers."*
> —Proverbs 17:6

> *"Honor thy father and mother; which is the first commandment with promise."*
> —Ephesians 6:2

You will probably be tempted in your adolescent years to rebel against your father and to disrespect him. May I encourage you not to yield to that temptation because all it will bring you is trouble. Whatever the situation with your dad, whether he does right or not, still honour him as your father, and you will be blessed for doing so. Here are some ways in which you can honour your father:

1. *Develop a relationship with him.* It does not have to be the perfect situation. Seek your father out if you have to, and sit down and talk with him. Go out to eat together, alone. Ask him questions about his history and the path that life has taken him. You will be amazed at how much you can learn from your father, how much he can help you, and how similar you both are.

2. *Listen to him.* God gives fathers a certain insight into

their children. Your father knows you very well, largely because he knows himself. The things that he tells you to avoid, listen to him, and avoid those things. The things that he tells you to do, listen to him, and do those things. Of course, everything your father tells you may not be good. Use discretion, and as they say, "eat the chicken and leave the bones."

3. *Respect your father*. No matter what has happened in the past or what is happening now, show respect to your father. I think a very good way to do this is by the way you address him. Please do not do as some young people do today and call your father by his first name. That, to me, is highly disrespectful. There is a saying in the black community—you would get "your teeth knocked out" for calling a parent by his or her first name. It will not kill you to say 'Yes, Sir' and 'No, Sir' when he speaks to you or asks you a question.

4. *Love your dad*. For some this is easier said than done. I say that because many young black men have been hurt because of painful past experiences regarding their dad. Here is how you can love your dad no matter what has taken place in the past—choose. Yes, you have a powerful tool and that tool is choice. First, you must choose to forgive. Second, you must choose to love your dad unconditionally. God will help you to do it, if you let Him.

Your relationship with your dad may not be perfect, and it probably never will be perfect because we are imperfect people, but it can be much better. YBM, if you would only do your part,

God will bless you for that. Don't worry about whether or not he is doing his part; you just do yours. God will take care of the rest.

Loving Dad,

Daniel

P.T.:

- Most fathers try to bring up their sons to be as good a man as they meant to be.
  —Selected

- My father gave me the greatest gift anyone could give another person, he believed in me.
  —Jim Valvano

- The father who does not teach his son his duties is equally guilty with the son who neglects them.
  —Selected

- My best training came from my father.
  —Woodrow Wilson

ON YOUR RELATIONSHIP WITH YOUR MOTHER

Letter Ten

Dear Y.B.M.:

"Honour thy father and <u>mother</u>; which is the first commandment with promise, that it may be well with thee, and thou mayest live long on the earth."

—Ephesians 6: 2-3

Throughout Black American history, the mother has played a critical leadership role in most black homes. There are many reasons for that and I don't have time or space to get into those reasons now. Suffice it to say, our dear black mothers have had to take on that strong leadership role. It was thrust upon them. Thank God somebody did take that role, otherwise Black America would be in worse shape than what it is in now.

Let me throw in, however, that it is a new day now, and it is time for black men to rise up, to take responsibility, and to take their God-given role as the head of their households. It is time, also, for our women to let them.

Be that as it may, what kind of relationship ought you to have with your mother? What are your responsibilities and obligations to her? No matter your family situation, here are some things God commands you to do and that you ought to do out of love:

1. *Respect your mother.* It does not matter your family situation; it does not matter what your mother has

done or what she has not done; it does not matter whether she was a good mother or the mother from hell—your responsibility is to respect her. You have to lay aside any negative emotions, forgive failures of the past, and show her respect. There is absolutely no excuse for a man to disrespect his mother.

One of the greatest lessons that you can learn in life is the principle of *authority*. When you fully understand the principle of authority, you will know that it doesn't matter what type of person the one in authority is; if they are in a God-given position of authority over you—in this case your parents—you had better respect them. I do not care if your mother is the biggest drunkard or whore in town, you had better respect her because she is still your mother, and if she is from the old school, she'll remind you of that fact. Here are some quick ways that you can show respect to your mother:

A. I am from the old school. I believe 'Yes, Ma'am' and 'No, Ma'am' are in order when addressing her.

B. Don't talk back! No matter how old you get, son, don't you ever talk back to your mother! You may be right in what you are saying, but don't talk back. When Momma is talking to you—trying to tell you something, don't talk back because black mothers still have the legal right to "knock your teeth out of your mouth." And please don't rare back as if you are going to hit her because you are sure in for a "butt-whipping" then. I know of grown football players who can still get their "butt" whipped by their mother. Don't mess with Momma.

C. Never call your mother by her first name. For old school mothers that's a sure backhand across your mouth without one word being said by her. Then she will give you the eyes—the look that says, 'I dare you to say that again.' Or, 'You had better think twice before you say anything else stupid.'

D. If you think your mother's lifestyle is out of order, just keep your mouth shut, leave her alone, and pray for her. It is not your place to correct your mother. If your mother is wrong about something in her life, she already knows what it is. She doesn't need a child, whose diapers she has changed, to tell her she is wrong. Don't get all upset. Leave her alone and trust God to fix whatever is wrong in her life. Besides, once a person is past forty years of age, only God can help them anyway.

2. *Listen to your mother.* Notice these verses from the Word of God:

"My son, hear the instruction of thy father, and forsake not the law of thy mother."
—Proverbs 1:8

"My son, keep thy father's commandments, and forsake not the law of thy mother."
—Proverbs 6:20

Listen to your mother. There are many valuable things that she can tell you as to how to deal with the problems of life.

After graduating from high school, I immediately left home and I have not lived under my parents' roof since then. That was over thirty years ago. I remember one of the last things my mother said to me via a note she wrote in my senior high school scrap book. It read: "Son, roll with the punches." So, when the punches of life started coming, I started rolling. You see, that is the law of my mother, and just remembering her words to me have helped me through many storms over the past thirty years or so.

Listen to your mother, son.

Now, after you are grown, and have left home, still respectfully listen to your mother, but make your own decisions with God's help because you are the one who will have to live with the consequences of those decisions. Your mother may not like that idea too much, but after a while, by and by, she will understand.

3. *Love your mother.* Love your mother unconditionally. This means to love her in spite of her faults. Love her in spite of past misunderstandings. Love her in spite of the fact that she cursed you out in front of the entire family

last Thanksgiving and said your girlfriend was not a beauty queen. Forget all of that and love her anyway.

Here are some ways that you can show that love:

a. Be a good son. Do good things with your life.

b. Don't be a financial drain on your mother—always asking her for money. Rather, when God blesses you, you give her some money. Most black mothers don't mind telling you that the cards and flowers are fine, but the money is better.

c. Tell her you love her. That will mean more to her than anything.

In closing this letter, let me kindly say, respect and love your mother. Listen to your mother as I have just delineated, but remember that God comes before your mother. That may be obvious, but from my role as a minister, I have learned that that needs to be said. Notice what Jesus had to say about this matter:

"He that loveth father or mother more than me is not worthy of me: and he that loveth son or daughter more than me is not worthy of me."
—Matthew 10:37

Sad to say, many black men have almost denied God's Word to the point where their mother's word means more to them than God's Word, and that is not the way it should be. At some point, friend, in a man's life, a mother has to release her son, and a son will have to let go of his mother. That is just the way God designed

83

for things to be. I share these simple truths because so many young black men have allowed their relationship with their mother to hinder their relationships with their wives and children; they have allowed their relationship with their mother to hurt their finances; they have allowed their relationship with their mother to affect them when they are making major decisions in life. This ought not so to be. To help us have the proper healthy relationship with our mothers, we must come to Jesus.

Jesus is the best example of how a man should relate to his mother after he is grown. Notice with me three principles that should guide us, as grown men, in relating to our mothers:

1. While Jesus was living under his parents' authority and roof, he submitted to their authority even though He was God. This goes back to the principle of authority. Notice this verse from the Word of God:

    "And he said unto them, How is it that ye sought me? Wist ye not that I must be about my Father's business? And they understood not the saying which he spake unto them. And he went down with them, and came to Nazareth, and was subject unto them: but his mother kept all these sayings in her heart."
    —Luke 2:49-51

2. When Jesus became grown and his mission in life was taking shape, his relationship with his mother took a marked turn. Jesus, being a man, took a more leadership position over his mother and his mother

took on a more supportive and encouraging role. Now it appears as though Jesus had to lovingly say and do some things to help His dear mother see this change in their relationship; for Mary, like all mothers, struggled with seeing her "baby" slipping away from her motherly grip. Notice with me two startling statements that Jesus had to strategically make to help His dear mother understand that there was a major change taking place in their relationship, and please notice, as a side point, that these two statements were made publicly:

"While he yet talked to the people, behold his mother and his brethren stood without, desiring to speak with him. Then one said unto him, Behold, thy mother and thy brethren stand without, desiring to speak with thee. But he answered and said unto him that told him, Who is my mother? And who are my brethren? And he stretched forth his hand toward his disciples, and said, behold my mother and my brethren! For whosoever shall do the will of my Father which is in heaven, the same is my brother, and sister, and mother."

—Matthew 12:46-50

"And the third day there was a marriage in Cana of Galilee; and the mother of Jesus was there: And both Jesus was called, and his disciples, to the marriage. And when they wanted wine, the mother of Jesus saith unto him, They have no wine. Jesus saith unto her, Woman, what have I to do with thee? Mine hour is not yet come. His mother saith unto the servant, Whatsoever he saith unto you, do it."

—John 2:1-5

Now some may think that Jesus was being disrespectful. He was not. His abruptness was by divine design, to lovingly help His dear mother realize that a change was taking place in their relationship. He was no longer the little, cuddly baby in the manger. He was a grown man with an extraordinary mission to not only save mankind, but to save her as well.

Jesus was basically saying, "Mama, I thank you for raising Me, but I am grown and in charge now, and it is now My turn to not only take care of you and lead you, but to lead the world to a higher level. Mama, you did your part, now it is time for Me to do My part. Mama, I love you. Mama, I respect you. Mama, I honour you, but Mama, I don't need to be trained any more. You have already trained Me. I don't need to be taught any more, for you have already taught Me. What I need from you, Mama, is for you to stand to the side, and love Me and cheer Me on. I need for you to back Me; to tell me you love Me, even though you may not understand what's going on. Mama, I can't run this ball that God has given Me with you in front of Me. However, if I know you are in the grandstand pulling for Me and loving Me and supporting Me, then I can save—not only you, but the entire world."

Now, brother, your dear mother is not going to care for this change too much because it is hard for a mother to carry a baby for nine months and watch him grow from an infant into a man and then see him become so independent; but the change in the relationship must take place. The proverbial "apron strings" must be cut and the only way to cut anything is abruptly.

If a mother has raised her son right, and the son handles the "apron cutting" ceremony right, then it is really a beautiful thing to behold in life when the big, ol', husky son who was once a seven pound baby becomes the leader, protector, provider, and, if you will, saviour of the mother. It is one of those beautiful pictures in life that God gives us.

3. The last thing that Jesus did was to take care of his mother. Even though a son ought to always respect and love his mother no matter what his age, the relationship must change. The relationship changes in such a way that it is almost like a reversal in the mother/son role. That is okay. as long as we respect and love our mothers. Notice this touching verse from St. John:

    "When Jesus therefore saw his mother, and the disciple standing by, whom he loved, he saith unto his mother, Woman, behold thy son! Then saith he to the disciple, Behold thy mother! And from that hour that disciple took her unto his own home."
    —John 19: 26-27

    Young black man, while Jesus was suffering on the cross, while He was about to die, while He was in the most excruciating pain, He made the extra effort to make sure that His mother would be taken care of after He was gone.

It is your responsibility and obligation to make sure your mother is cared for after her productive years are over.

Show respect and love to your mother, and don't be afraid to cut the "apron strings" when it is time to do so. God expects you to do all of that.

Loving My Mother,

Daniel

P.T.:

■   The greatest lessons I ever learned were on my mother's knees.
—Abraham Lincoln

■   The art of mothering is to teach the art of living to children.
—Elain Heffner

■   History shows almost all the greatest workers for God had godly mothers.
—Selected

ON YOUR RELATIONSHIP WITH YOUR DAUGHTER

Letter Eleven

Dear Y.B.M.:

In this letter, I would like to speak with you about your relationship with your daughters. I do not think there is a sweeter relationship on God's earth than the relationship of a father and his daughter. When I think of my daughters, I think of sunshine, joy, smiles, blessings, and happiness. My daughters can lift my spirits more than anything or anyone on earth can. If I allow myself to do so, I could very easily become the proverbial father that is wrapped around his little girls' fingers.

Notice with me the great value of a daughter. Besides your wife, no one can comfort you and cheer you like your daughter. Throughout your life you will find that: (1) She will be there for her father even when no one else will be there; and that (2) There is a special love in her heart for her father that, often times, cannot be shaken by anyone or anything. As her father, you have the opportunity to help shape her and mold her into being a great woman of God, as well as a great wife and mother, because you can give her some advice on these things from a perspective that her mother cannot. In you, she can see what a husband and father should be. Below are some positive things that you can do in order to have a good relationship with your daughter or daughter to be:

1. **Hug her often.** She really needs that. There is an old saying that goes like this: "Hug her or someone else will." That usually ends up to be true.

2. **From time to time, take her out, and spend time alone with her.** Your daughter will remember and cherish those experiences long after she is grown and on her own.

3. **Love and treat her mother right.** The way you treat her mother will make a lasting impression on her, and will help her in her relationhip with her future husband.

4. **Your daughter will probably have a tendency to try to manipulate you. Be loving toward her but firm at the same time.** Don't let her get away with disobedience, bad attitudes, and selfishness just because she is a girl. Teach her the great lesson of obedience from an early age.

5. **Teach her the things of the Lord** so that when she grows up and has to face the world alone, she will already know to lean on the Lord.

6. **Tell her you love her often.** One of the greatest gifts that a father can give his daughter is a sense of love, belonging, and security.

The relationship between you and your daughter can be a tremendous blessing. Do your part to make it happen.

Thanking God for my Daughters,

Daniel

P.T.:

■ Certain is it that there is no kind of affection so purely angelic as of a father to a daughter. In love to our wives there is desire; to our sons, ambition; but to our daughters there is something which there are no words to express.

—Joseph Addison

■ Let your daughter have, first of all, the book of Psalms for holiness of heart, and be instructed in the Proverbs of Solomon for her godly life.

—St. Jerome

■ The most important thing that a father can do for his children is to love their mother.

—Theodore Hesburg

ON YOUR RELATIONSHIP WITH YOUR SONS

Letter Twelve

Dear Y.B.M.:

In this letter, I would like to say some things to you regarding your son or son to be. The greatest gift that you will ever receive in this life will be the gift of children. Even though you will love all of your children just the same, your daughters will hold a very special place in your heart, and although in a different way, your son or sons will hold a very special place in your heart as well.

Do not take having a son lightly. This is a very special gift in your life. Here are some of the benefits of having a son: (a) He will carry on your name; (b) He will carry on the, hopefully, positive things that you instill in him; (c) He will more than likely carry on your resemblance so that when people see him, they see you; (d) He will teach what you have taught him.

Here are some suggestions as to what you ought to do with your son:

1. **Pray with him and for him daily.** I am happy to say, that by the grace of God, there has not been a day that my sons have not seen me pray.

2. **Spend lots of time alone with him.** As you know, there is this running controversy, as to whether or not parents should spend quality time or quantity time with their children. In my opinion, you really cannot spend

quality time without quantity time. Therefore, I have chosen to live a lifestyle that would allow me to be there for my children. You can't just fit your children into your schedule. Your children are your life. Sometimes your children just need to see you there in the house.

3. **Talk with him. Really talk with him.** Get into your son's head, and let him get into yours. What I have found helpful, when I am with my sons, is to talk about something that is interesting to both of us.

4. **Teach him biblical principles, and give him wise counsel regarding life.** The best thing I have ever done with my sons, and all of my children, for that matter, is to read the Bible all the way through with them, and teach them the principles therein. I strongly encourage you to do the same. Basically, all you have to do is read three chapters a day. Try it. It will change your life and his life as well. But, don't just read the Scriptures — do the Scriptures. Obey the Scriptures yourself and be a great example to your sons. The Bible says: *"Train up a child in the way he should go: and when he is old, he will not depart from it"* (Proverbs 22:6).

5. **Work it out so he gets the best education possible.** My wife and I felt the best way to raise our children was to homeschool them. We have homeschooled all seven of our children since birth. You may have chosen another route, but whatever you do, give your son and daughter the best possible education that you can. This will bode well for them and for you throughout their lifetime.

6. **Play with him.** While growing up, I played quarterback on one of my high school football teams. When my sons and I go exercising, we always take a football. They play as my receivers. We have a lot of fun together. I share with my sons this life principle: *work hard and then play hard.*

7. **Be genuinely interested in what he does and what he is interested in.** Help him develop his gifts. Find out what your son is good at and encourage him to become the best he can be.

8. **Praise him for his good accomplishments, and encourage him where he may be failing.** All of us know the value and power of praise. I use it lavishly on my sons when they do well. But, I also rebuke them and chastise them when I know they are not doing their best.

9. **Chastise him swiftly and firmly.** Teach him one of the most important lessons of life, and that is, the lesson of obedience. I cannot emphasize this enough: love your sons, so much so, that you will chastise them when they are disobedient. The Bible says to: *"Chasten thy son while there is hope, and let not thy soul spare for his crying"* (Proverbs 19:18).

10. **Teach him good manners and respect.** There is nothing wrong with your sons saying "yes sir" and "no sir" to you and to others who are much older than they are.

11. **When he is old enough give him this book.**

95

12. **Teach him how to be a loving, but strong leader, as a man.** We have too many men today, who are soft when they need to be firm, and too many men who are firm when they need to be gentle. Teach him how to balance the two.

13. **Love him and tell him so often.** It won't take away from his manliness. Don't hesitate to let your sons know you love them, and don't hesitate to tell them how much you love them.

Spend quality and quantity time with your son and/or sons and it will pay invaluable dividends for you, him, your family, and for society as well.

Raising a great son for the glory of God,

Daniel

P.T.:

- My father said, 'Politics asks the question: Is it expedient? Vanity asks: Is it popular? But conscience asks: Is it right?'
  —Dexter Scott King

- By profession I am a soldier and take pride in that fact. But I am prouder - infinitely prouder - to be a father. A soldier destroys in order to build; the father only builds, never destroys. The one has the potentiality of death;

the other embodies creation and life. And while the hordes of death are mighty, the battalions of life are mightier still. It is my hope that my son, when I am gone, will remember me not from the battle field but in the home repeating with him our simple daily prayer, 'Our Father who art in Heaven.'

—Douglas Macarthur

■ If the past cannot teach the present and the father cannot teach the son, then history need not have bothered to go on, and the world has wasted a great deal of time.

—Russell Hoban

■ What a father says to his children is not heard by the world, but it will be heard by posterity.

—Jean Paul Richter

ON YOUR RELATIONSHIP WITH YOUR SISTER

Letter Thirteen

Dear Y.B.M.:

I trust that you are doing well.

I am dropping you a note regarding your relationship with your sister. You have probably noticed that the older you both get, the more you see things differently because you are both maturing, not only physically, but mentally, emotionally, and spiritually, if you are saved, as well. Although my sisters and I do not see eye-to-eye on several things, I still love them and pray for them daily. Be that as it may, here are some things that will make you an asset and a blessing to your sister while you both are growing up:

1. **Pray for her daily.**

2. **Talk with her if she is open to talking with you.** If she doesn't want to talk, leave her alone, but still love her.

3. **As she grows older, warn her about the intentions of most men.** Not only should you warn her, you should protect her, if you can.

4. **Love her unconditionally,** and let her grow into what God wants her to be.

5. **Respect her.** Respect her privacy. Give her room.

As you can see, I don't have much to say about the relationship with your sisters. Normally, after high school, maybe college, each of you both begin to do your own thing, including having different friends. But keep the doors of communication open and stay in touch with your sister or sisters. Believe it or not, you may need one another one day.

Looking out for our sisters,

Daniel

P.T.:

■ As we grew up, my brothers acted like they didn't care, but I always knew they looked out for me and were there!
—Catherine Pulsifer

■ Our brothers and sisters are there with us from the dawn of our personal stories to the inevitable dusk.
—Susan Scarf Merrell

■ You don't choose your family. They are God's gift to you, as you are to them.
—Desmond Tutu

ON YOUR RELATIONSHIP WITH YOUR BROTHER

Letter Fourteen

Dear Y.B.M.:

Maybe as young boys you fought and often times did not get along as brothers should. But as brothers, you will find that as you grow older, oftentimes, the relationship can grow to become one of the most special on earth. Your relationship can turn out to be more than just brothers; you can become very close friends. Here are some ideas to help enhance that relationship and keep it growing:

1. **Remember, even though you are brothers, you are both independent and more different than you think.**

2. **Genuinely respect his differences and opinions.** Let him be him and you be you. For example, when my little brother got married, I shared something with him, but, I was quick to tell him that he had to put his twist on what I had shared with him.

3. **Do not compete against your brother.** That is asinine activity. Forget this stuff called sibling rivalry. Just do your best in whatever field you are in, and encourage him to do his thing.

4. **Be completely candid and real in all of your dealings with your brother.** He knows when you are

putting on. He knows better than most when you are not real.

5. **Stay in touch, but not too much.** Give him time and room to grow, if you have that kind of relationship.

6. **Challenge and encourage him to do better and greater things with his life**, and to strive for spiritual gain instead of material gain.

7. **Most of all, love him unconditionally, and stick by him through the good times and the bad times.** Don't be condemning, rather be encouraging.

Other than my relationship with my wife, I do not think I have had a more close family relationship than with my brother, Mark. Even though my brother and I are not as close as we used to be, I enjoyed those times we used to spend together. It was so amazing how even though we were years apart in age, we saw the world basically in the same way. I wish you and your brother would share such a relationship for at least some time in your adult life.

With Brotherly Love,

Daniel

P.T.:

- There's no other love like the love for a brother. There's no other love like the love from

102

a brother.

—Astrid Alauda

■ Sometimes being a brother is even better than being a superhero.

—Mark Brown

■ Blessed is the servant who loves his brother as much when he is sick and useless as when he is well and can be of service to him. And blessed is he who loves his brother as well when he is afar off as when he is by his side, and who would say nothing behind his back he might not, in love, say before his face.

—St. Francis of Assisi

ON YOUR RELATIONSHIP WITH YOUR FRIENDS

Letter Fifteen

Dear Y.B.M.:

May I say a word to you about friends. What would we do without our friends? Even the Bible speaks about friends:

"A man that hath friends must shew himself friendly: and there is a friend that sticketh closer than a brother."
—Proverbs 18:24

To me there are different degrees of friendship:

1. *Friends on the periphery.* These are friends who really don't know the real you; you know one another at a distance.

2. *Friends in the middle.* These are people who you see more often, but you have not allowed them into the inner circle of your life.

3. *Friends in the inner circle.* These are those who know you and who know you well; you know them and you know them well. You also love one another unconditionally. When the winds and storms of life blow, others will run, but these friends will stick and stay.

Here are some things that you can do to create and maintain good, strong friendships:

a. This may shock you, but don't seek friends—let God give you the friends that He wants you to have.

b. Listen to friends, but think for yourself. Don't allow your friends to think for you.

c. Work at being friendly yourself. Remember Proverbs 18:24: *"A man that hath friends must shew himself friendly: and there is a friend that sticketh closer than a brother."*

d. Forget trying to be popular and having a bunch of friends. You will find in life there will only be a few who turn out to be your "ace-boon-coons"; that is, a *"friend that sticketh closer than a brother."* So, work at developing strong relationships with these friends.

e. Allow your friends to have friends that are not your friends. I am a firm believer that just because Joe is your friend, he doesn't have to be my friend.

f. Come through for your friends. When the winds and storms of life come in your friends' lives, be there for them. Whatever it takes, be there for them. "You reap what you sow."

Be a *Friend That Sticketh Closer Than a Brother,*

Daniel

P.T.:

■ Friendship is born at that moment when one person says to another, 'What! You too? I thought I was the only one.'

—C.S. Lewis

■ A friend is someone who understands your past, believes in your future, and accepts you just the way you are.

—Author Unknown

■ He is your friend who pushes you nearer to God.

—Selected

■ True friends stab you in the front.

—Selected

ON YOUR RELATIONSHIP WITH YOUR GRANDPARENTS

Letter Sixteen

Dear Y.B.M.:

I hope that you are doing well, today.

This morning, I would like to mention to you the great value of your grandparents. If your grandparents are living, you have a tremendous treasure in your life. If you have great grandparents you have a greater treasure. Sit down and talk with your grandparents. Some of the most intriguing conversations that I have ever had have been with my grandfather and my two grandmothers. They are my link to the past as to how it really was "back when", and also they are a great help to my knowing who I am and where I came from. Here are some things you can do to reap jewels from your ancestors:

1. **Go and talk with them when they are not preoccupied with other things.** Sometimes, visit them alone, if you can.

2. **Listen, Listen, Listen.** You are not there to talk that much, but you are there to learn all that you can. Your grandparents can really give you an education.

3. **Show respect to them.** No matter what kind of lifestyle they have had, there is nothing wrong with saying "Yes, Sir" and "No, Ma'am." They may move slower, talk slower, think slower, have different views about life, but

you owe them that respect.

4. **Do not go with the attitude that they can't tell you anything because they did not attain the educational level that you have.** They still have more knowledge and wisdom in their little finger than you have in your little brain.

5. **Eat the chicken and leave the bones.** Grandparents don't speak ex-cathedra simply because they are grandparents. Everything they say is not necessarily right.

6. **Tell your grandparents you love them and show your appreciation for them.**

Your grandparents can be a great blessing and help to you if you let them.

Linking up with your personal past,

Daniel

P.T.:

■ The history of our grandparents is remembered not with rose petals but in the laughter and tears of their children and their children's children. It is into us that the lives of grandparents have gone. It is in us that their history becomes a future.
—Charles & Ann Morse

■   Grandparents and grandchildren, together
. they create a chain of love, linking the past,
with the future. The chain may lengthen, but
it will never part.

—Author Unknown

■   Most of the successful people I've known are
the ones who do more listening than talking.

—Bernard Baruch

ON YOUR RELATIONSHIP WITH YOUR CHILDREN STILL

Letter Seventeen

Dear Y.B.M.:

I hope that you are listening to your grandparents.

In this letter, I want to talk with you about something that many people do not like to discuss with young black men, but something that needs to be addressed—that is the subject of children before marriage. If you are not married, do not engage in the activity that causes children to come before marriage. If however, you already have children outside of marriage, may I say a word to you regarding that:

First, *people sometimes call the child born out of wedlock, illegitimate.* In my opinion, it is not the child that is illegitimate; the parents are the ones who are illegitimate. If you had a child out of wedlock, you ought not to be proud of it; rather, you ought to confess your sin before God, get things right before Him, and do right by the mother and the child.

Second, *if you love the young lady and feel that she is to be your wife, then you ought to make plans to marry her.* (I didn't say marry her immediately, for that may be impossible or impractical at this point; I said make earnest plans to marry her.) Please do not rush and marry her to cover up your guilt or to try to cover up what you both did. If you both know that you are not right for one another as far as marriage goes, then do not marry because life will be nothing but hell and misery for both of you and the child.

Third, *whatever you both decide, sit down at some point, and speak frankly and honestly with her parents about your intentions.* Apologize to them, but don't let them talk you into marrying their daughter if you know beyond any shadow of a doubt that she is not the one for you.

Fourth, *do not consent to an abortion.* You will regret it the rest of your life. (You may not have control over her decision, but you do not have to be a partaker in her wrong doing.) Remember, friend, you may have control over the sexual act, but you do not have control over life. You do not give life, only God does!

Fifth, *do whatever it takes to take care of the child.* You may not be able to support the child fully as you would like. Get yourself a job, if you do not already have one, and be a financial support each month, if you can.

Sixth, *if the young lady you had the baby with becomes seriously involved with another man, or gets engaged or married, you need to respect that man as the stepfather of your child* and do unto him as you would like for a man to do unto you if you were in the same situation. In other words, if he wants to take care of that young lady and the child and he doesn't want you to support or come around, because he feels that it would cause problems, then respect the man of that house and leave them alone, until they give you permission to see the child. Before you get all upset, remember that you didn't marry her, so she really does not have to answer to you in any way, shape, form, or fashion.

Seventh, *whether your child is with you or not, pray daily for him or her.*

Eighth, *if you can spend time with the child, then spend as much time as you can with him or her.*

Ninth, *if you are at a distance from your child, write him or her monthly.* It will be a great encouragement to him or her during this difficult time in his or her life. As he or she grows older, he or she will never forget those letters.

Tenth, *tell your children that you love them often.*

Eleventh, *admit your sin and mistake and encourage and teach your sons not to do the same thing.*

Twelfth, if you get married to another woman, *make your child feel a part of the family,* for he or she is a part of the family.

Take Care of all Your Children,

Daniel

P.T.:

■   A baby is God's opinion that the world should go on.
—Carl Sandburg

■   Could I climb to the highest place in Athens, I would lift my voice and proclaim—fellow citizens, why do you turn and scrape every stone to gather wealth, and take so little care of your children, to whom one day you must relinquish it all?

—Socrates

■ To nourish children and raise them against odds is in any time, any place, more valuable than to fix bolts in cars or design nuclear weapons.

—Marilyn French

■ It is a wise father that knows his own child.

—William Shakespeare

ON YOUR LIFE AND RACE

RACISM IN AMERICA IS ALIVE AND WELL

Letter Eighteen

Dear Y.B.M.:

I trust that you have great relationships in your life.

Things are changing a little in light of Barack Obama running for the presidential office. However, racism, for the average black man in America, is still a reality and she ain't going nowhere. You need to hear that in the raw because it is true, very true, and because there are many who will not impart to you that truth.

While I was growing up, no one, straight out, told me that racism still existed. It wasn't until I was a grown man did I fully realize that racism and prejudice were still around and deeply rooted in the American society. Do not believe the lie that race relations are getting better. They are not! In fact, they are getting worse and more subtle, and will continue to get worse. Get it in your head: RACISM IS ALIVE AND WELL AND SHE AIN'T GOING NOWHERE! Why is racism here to stay? Here are some things you need to understand:

First, *racism is rooted in pride which is rooted in sin, which is rooted in the hearts of all men*, be they black, white, red or yellow. Jeremiah tells us in Jeremiah 17:9: ***"The heart is deceitful above all things, and desperately wicked: who can know it?"***

Racism is insidious. Although a man may not look like a racist on the outside, he may very well be a racist on the inside. And there is nothing that anybody can do to change another man on the inside.

Second, *you need to understand firmly, that this thing called racism, is not confined to the white man.* It has its grips on the black man as well. This means that you, yes, you, may even be a racist yourself. Surprised?

Third, *racism may not be the hatred of another race as many believe.* Racism is simply pride, somehow foolishly thinking, "because I am white or because I am black, or because I am Latino, I am better. I don't really hate anybody, I just think that my race is superior."

Fourth, *there is only one real solution to the sin problem of racism and that is the sin-bearer—Jesus Christ.* Only Jesus Christ can change a man's heart from hate to love and from pride to humility. Even after he has allowed Jesus Christ to come into his heart, he will have to allow God to crucify his pride daily.

Racism is here to stay. You will probably have to deal with it from both sides, for the rest of your life, but thank God there is hope, and that progress is taking place.

Fighting Racism from the Inside Out,

Daniel

P.T.:

- If I were you, I would stand for something,

I would count for something, and no man would push me around because my skin is black or his eyes are blue. I would stand for something. I would count.

—Dr. Benjamin E. Mays

■ You don't fight racism with racism, the best way to fight racism is with solidarity.

—Bobby Seale

■ I refuse to accept the view that mankind is so tragically bound to the starless midnight of racism and war that the bright daybreak of peace and brotherhood can never become a reality...I believe that unarmed truth and unconditional love will have the final word.

—Martin Luther King, Jr.

■ Racism is man's gravest threat to man— the maximum of hatred for a minimum of reason.

—Abraham Joshua Heschel

HOW TO DEAL WITH YOUR OWN RACISM, BITTERNESS, RESENTMENT AND ANGER

Letter Nineteen

Dear Y.B.M.:

I mentioned to you in my last letter, that you, a black man, could very well have some racism and prejudice in you. It is quite possible that you are a racist because you are a sinner like the rest of us.

Let me share a little story with you about how I became aware of some hidden racism and prejudice in my own heart. You might be asking, you, Daniel Whyte, a black man and a Christian? Yes, me, Daniel Whyte, a black man and a Christian—had to acknowledge some prejudice and racism in my own heart at one point in my life.

I was asked to speak in a meeting in southern California. It was a mixed audience—Whites, Blacks, and Latinos. A Latino was scheduled to speak before I was to speak. As this Latino brother rose to speak, this thought immediately crossed my wretched heart and mind: "What can this Latino, who probably got over here illegally, with his no alien card self and his broken English, tell us Blacks and Whites?" As soon as that thought finished its wicked course, God smote my heart and pointed out my own prejudice. You see, I did not have any prejudice toward the white folk who were there because they spoke proper English and because they had been here since the inception of America. My racism was toward those who were different then we were

("We", meaning Black and White American-born, English-speaking people). It was against those who I somehow thought I had an advantage over, those who I pridefully thought I was better than, simply because I was born here and spoke the English language. You see, I didn't really hate this Latino, I just thought I was better than him. And that is all racism is: thinking you are better than another, because you are in the majority or because you were here first, etc.

Could it be, dear young black man, that you have racism in your heart? No, you may not have this racist feeling toward whites, for some strange reason, but you have it toward Koreans, Indians or Latinos. That feeling of pride, that wicked feeling of superiority that you have regarding these other minority groups is the same feeling many Whites have about you. When you get up to speak, with no real effort of their own, many whites have the same thoughts that I had: "What can he tell us white people?" It is not really that they hate you, it is just that for whatever reason, they think that they are better than you; that they are superior to you.

To be looked upon that way is degrading, isn't it? It makes you feel bad and frustrated, doesn't it? It makes you feel as though you are always under the gun to do 200-percent better than your white counterpart, doesn't it? Well, guess how that Latino or Korean feels when you do them the same way? Here are some things that you can do to overcome your own racism:

First, admit and confess your sin of pride and racism or prejudice and thinking yourself better than others.

Second, see and treat all men with dignity, love, respect and without partiality. Always remember, what you dole out comes back to you triple-fold.

Third, do not come down on those less fortunate than you because those more fortunate than you have come down upon you. In other words, just because one race treats you badly, you should not treat another race of people the same way.

You will find that understanding and dealing with your own racism and prejudice will help you deal with the racism of others.

Loving Everybody,

Daniel

P.T.:

■ One day our descendants will think it incredible that we paid so much attention to things like the amount of melanin in our skin or the shape of our eyes or our gender instead of the unique identities of each of us as complex human beings.

—Franklin Thomas

■ Don't hold to anger, hurt or pain. They steal your energy and keep you from love.

—Selected

BLACK ON BLACK RACISM

Letter Twenty

Dear Y.B.M.:

I hope that you have overcome your own racism or prejudice.

I am writing at this time to share something with you that may sound a bit strange, and that is, how to deal with black on black prejudice. It is amazing how that many of us get so upset at the prejudice of Whites, but hardly ever say anything about the prejudice that we often have toward one another in our own race.

What is this black on black prejudice anyway? This phenomenon has raised its ugly head during the Obama campaign for president. It is when you, as a Black man, have any disdain for anything that is run, controlled, operated, or serviced by Black people. It is when you have this stupid something in your head that says "White is right," or at least better than Black, and you count everything that Blacks do as second best or second rate simply because it is done by Blacks. This reminds me of an old story an old saint shared with me. He said that back in his day they would joke about this phenomenon by saying the White man's ice was colder than the Black man's ice.

This kind of prejudice is evidenced in a Black picking a White lawyer over a Black lawyer, or a White doctor over a Black doctor, or a White dentist over a Black dentist. It is also evidenced in how many Blacks would rather deal with Whites often times in some of the more common areas of life; for example, waiting to deal with a White cashier over a Black cashier. Let me not fail to mention here, that probably the most painful one for our Black sisters is the Black man who thinks that the White woman is better than the Black woman.

Why are we prejudiced against our own people? First, we have bought into the subtle lie from this society that White is right, White is smarter, and White is better. Second, we watch too much television where Whites are often times seen as the heroes and the stars, and Blacks are seen as buffoons. Third, because many of us as blacks have bought into the lie that White is better, we actually do not strive for professionalism or excellence in our businesses and professions. It is in fact true that some Blacks have given other Blacks a bad name because they do not handle business in a professional maner. Fourth, some Blacks are so immature, petty and envious that they cannot stand to see another Black do well—the proverbial crab effect. Unfortunately, we have seen some of this in the Obama presidential campaign.

Dear young black man, overcome this strange prejudice against your own people by doing the following:

1. Accept the fact that all people are on level ground, even your people.

2. Those blacks who are not striving for excellence and professionalism in their respective jobs, challenge them in a loving way to do better.

3. Visit more black owned and operated businesses and professions.

4. If you go into business for yourself, or become a professional person, or even a cashier, treat all people with respect and dignity—even your own people.

Doing Away with Black on Black Prejudice,

Daniel

P.T.:

■   A sure way for someone to lift himself up is by helping to lift someone else.
—Booker T. Washington

■   The African race is a rubber ball. The harder you dash it to the ground, the higher it will rise.
—African Proverb

■   As you seek your way in the world, never fail to find a way to serve your community. Use your education and your success in life to help those still trapped in cycles of poverty and violence.
—Colin L. Powell

THE GOOD WHITE PEOPLE

Letter Twenty-One

Dear Y.B.M.:

As I write to you about how to handle prejudice and racism in this great country of ours, allow me to quickly say here, that if God blesses you with some good white friends, give Him thanks. Just as there are bad white people and bad black people for that matter, there are also some good white people in this country.

Don't let anybody fool you, if it had not been for the Lord using some good white folks behind the scenes, many successful and notable black people would not have attained the success they have attained. Wait a minute before you take that as a negative statement. It is a true statement—many of the notable black people in this country, past and present, did not necessarily pull themselves up by their own bootstraps. Some have, but most have had some help from some good black people and some good white people. Watch this:

1. Harriet Tubman had much help from some good white people on the underground railroad.

2. What would Frederick Douglass have done without his white abolitionist supporters?

3. Thank God for the good white people in Phillis Wheatley's life.

4. Would slavery have ended if it had not been for the force of William Wilberforce?

5. Would Spelman College and Morehouse College had so superbly educated our brightest and best, including Martin Luther King, Jr., without some good white people? By the way, these historically black colleges are named after some good white people who made these fine institutions possible.

6. Even though Martin Luther King, Jr. led the way in the Civil Rights movement, there were many good white people who stood behind him and supported him with their prayers, presence, money, and some even with their lives.

7. And finally, where would Barack Obama be with his historical run for the presidency without millions of good white people supporting him, against all odds?

Dear Y.B.M., please do not get into the mindset that all white people are out to get you. Even though I would encourage you to be "wise as a serpent, but harmless as a dove", when it comes to racism and prejudice in this country, be open to God using some good white people in your life, to open some doors for you that otherwise would not be open, and vice-versa.

Thank God for the good white people.

Yours for being wise,

Daniel

P.T.:

- We know all too little about the factors that affect the attitudes of the peoples of the world toward one another. It is clear, however, that color and race are at once the most important and the most enigmatic.

—John Hope Franklin

- A fully functional multiracial society cannot be achieved without a sense of history and open, honest dialogue.

—Cornel West

- I hope that people will finally come to realize that there is only one 'race' - the human race - and that we are all members of it.

—Margaret Atwood

WINNING OVER RACISM

Letter Twenty-Two

Dear Y.B.M.:

I trust that you are treating your brothers and sisters *"according to the flesh"* more kindly and with dignity and respect, and I also hope that you are mature enough to allow God to give you some good white friends to help you down the road on this most difficult journey.

It has been established that racism is firmly entrenched in this society. Frankly speaking, I believe racism will be here with us until the end. Here is how you can win over racism:

First, the best thing to do is ignore it and avoid it. One of the best things you can do for a racist White man or Black man, for that matter, is ignore him. Just leave him alone.

Second, do not get ruffled by racist/prejudiced people. If you get ruffled now, you will be getting ruffled the rest of your life. Always be cool, calm, and collected, as they say.

Third, "turn the other cheek". Believe it or not, it works. It is kind of hard to fight a man who does not want to fight.

Fourth, do not allow yourself to become bitter. I repeat: do not allow yourself to become bitter. That is exactly what White racists want you to do—become bitter, angry and frustrated, because they know that you render yourself ineffective when you become bitter. Don't let them get into your head like that. They know that a man who is filled with anger or bitterness cannot function or prosper that way.

Fifth, remember all White people are not racist or prejudice. Do not try to deal with the White community as a whole, but deal with each person on an individual basis. Treat them as you would like for them to treat you.

Sixth, become independent through knowledge and by having your own source of income, thus not putting yourself in a situation where you can be subject to racism.

Seventh, there are many dear White people who are not racist or prejudice; they simply do not understand some things. Take the time to help educate these good-hearted people in this matter.

Eighth, do not take racism too seriously. It is probably not that important of a matter right now. We can spend our energy in more productive ways.

Ninth, rioting, fighting, burning, and raising hell is not the way to deal with racism. All that does is drive the root of racism deeper. Avoid such asinine activities.

You can win over racism if you use your head and your heart.

Winning Over Racism and Prejudice,

Daniel

P.T.:

■   I would be nothing else in God's creation but a black man.

—Marcus Garvey

■   I find in being black, a thing of beauty; a joy; a strength; a secret cup of gladness.

—Ossie Davis

ON BECOMING COLOR-BLIND

Letter Twenty-Three

Dear Y.B.M.:

I trust that you are winning over racism.

In this short note, I would like to say a word to you about becoming color-blind.

America is a multicultural society. America is not just made up of white and black, but of all colors, races, nationalities, and tongues. If you are going to be a leader in this country, you had better shed your "black thing" mentality and become color-blind in your dealings with all people. To help you with this concept, here are some suggestions:

1. I have had the privilege of traveling all over the world, and believe it or not, all people are basically the same. No matter where they come from, or what language they speak, all people desire the same things, for the most part.

2. Learn how to speak the universal language of love. You must develop a loving heart for all people. Smile and shake hands. They are just as afraid of you as you are of them.

3. Show an interest in other people's culture and ways. Ask them questions. Learn a few words of their language. Eat their food. (By the way, I would strongly encourage you to learn how to speak Spanish and Chinese fluently, in light of the new, global economy.)

4. When you get the opportunity, please travel as much as you can. You will get a perspective on life that you can't get any other way. From traveling, you will understand what I mean when I say, all people are basically the same.

5. If you can't travel, please take the time to read about other people and their way of life. There are many good videos out that will help you become more cosmopolitan.

I hope you will learn quickly this valuable lesson, and that is, people are really just people.

Yours for being Color-blind and
at the Same Time Keeping it Real,

Daniel

P.T.:

■ It is never too late to give up our prejudices.
—Henry David Thoreau

■ Prejudice is opinion without judgement.
—Selected

■ Until justice is blind to color, until education is unaware of race, until opportunity is unconcerned with the color of men's skins, emancipation will be a proclamation but not a fact.
—Lyndon B. Johnson

ON YOUR LIFE
AND THIS AND THAT

PROVERBS FOR YOUNG MEN
TO LIVE BY

Letter Twenty-Four

Dear Y.B.M.:

Over the years, the Book of Proverbs in the Bible, has been a book that has helped me with many practical things in this life. May I encourage you to read this book at least twice a year. The Book of Proverbs has thirty-one chapters. Why not get into the habit of reading one chapter a day? The truths contained therein will help you greatly in your life. Here are just some of the key verses that have been a great help to me over the years:

"A wise man will hear, and will increase learning, and a man of understanding shall attain unto wise counsels."
—Proverbs 1:5

"Trust in the Lord with all thine heart; and lean not unto thine own understanding. In all thy ways acknowledge him, and he shall direct thy paths."
—Proverbs 3:5-6

"Honour the Lord with thy substance, and with the first fruits of all thine increase: so shall thy barns be filled with plenty, and thy presses shall burst out with new wine."
—Proverbs 3:9-10

"Keep thy heart with all diligence; for out of it are the issues of life."
—Proverbs 4:23

"Let thy fountain be blessed: and rejoice with the wife of thy youth."

—Proverbs 5:16

"Go to the ant thou sluggard; consider her ways, and be wise."

—Proverbs 6:6

"Can a man take fire in his bosom and his clothes not be burned?"

—Proverbs 6:27

"Lying lips are abomination to the Lord: but they that deal truly are his delight."

—Proverbs 12:22

"Whoso findeth a wife findeth a good thing, and obtaineth favour of the Lord."

—Proverbs 18:22

"Give instruction to a wise man, and he will be yet wiser: teach a just man, and he will increase in learning."

—Proverbs 9:9

"When a man's ways please the Lord, he maketh even his enemies to be at peace with him."

—Proverbs 16:7

"Better is little with the fear of the Lord than great treasure and trouble therewith."

—Proverbs 15:16

"How much better is it to get wisdom than gold! and to get understanding rather to be chosen than silver!"
—Proverbs 16:16

Dear brother, just read the book of Proverbs, and be blessed. There are hundreds of other Proverbs that can help make you a grand success in life.

Yours from Proverbsville,

Daniel

P.T.:

■   Bible reading is an education in itself.
—Lord Tennyson

■   Some people like to read so many [Bible] chapters every day. I would not dissuade them from the practice, but I would rather lay my soul asoak in half a dozen verses all day than rinse my hand in several chapters. Oh, to be bathed in a text of Scripture, and to let it be sucked up in your very soul, till it saturates your heart!
—Charles Haddon Spurgeon

■   Reading the Bible without meditating on it is like trying to eat without swallowing.
—Anonymous

WHEN THIS LIFE IS OVER

Letter Twenty-Five

Dear Y.B.M.:

I am writing to you this time about the end of your life. I read a book recently entitled: *7 Habits of Highly Successful People*. In that book, the author mentioned the phrase: "Begin with the end in mind." When you think about it, that is a very powerful principle for all of us to keep in mind. When you are lying in that grave, what would your life have meant? What would you have accomplished worthwhile? What, if anything worthwhile, would you have left behind? May I encourage you as that book encouraged me, to "begin with the end in mind". Here are some things that you can do each day so that you can have a good ending as well as a good beginning:

First, live each day with God in mind. A good way to do this is to pray every day, read your Bible every day, and meditate upon the Lord every day. I can honestly say that ever since I met the Lord Jesus Christ as my Saviour on December 19, 1979, the Lord has been on my mind.

Second, live with others in mind. Do not live a life of self-centeredness, but live a life for others, helping others, serving others, caring for others, and pulling others out of the fire.

Third, live out your passion! Live out your passion! Live out your passion! Live out your passion! Don't allow yourself to get locked into something that God didn't make you to do. Do only what God made you to do, do only what you love to do, and do it with all your might!

Fourth, write a journal of various events and places and people that were connected with your life. Leave it behind for your children and grandchildren to read so they will know more about you. You may also write a few words of wisdom for them. This will be a great joy to them as they begin their young life.

Fifth, please try to leave some money and property behind for your family. I am amazed how many fathers die and leave nothing behind which their children can get started.

Sixth, I will remind you again to make sure that you are saved, because the Bible says, *"After death the judgement."* If you are not sure that you are saved, here is how you can know for sure:

First of all, **understand that you are a sinner like the rest of us.** Yes, believe it or not, each of us born into this world has sinned. Each one of us has broken the laws of God. The Bible states plainly: *"For all have sinned and come short of the glory of God"* (Romans 3:23).

Second, **God wants us to understand that because of our sin, there is a great punishment and that punishment is death — both spiritual death and physical death.** You see, because of sin, we not only die physically, but also because of sin we die spiritually. This spiritual death is actually eternal separation from God in a place called Hell. Notice what God's Word says about this death: *"For the wages of sin is death…"* (Romans 6:23).

"But the fearful, and unbelieving, and the abominable, and murderers and whoremongers, and sorcerers, and idolaters, and all liars, shall have their part in the lake which burneth with fire and brimstone: which is the second death."

—Revelation 21:8

Third, **after realizing our sad and condemned condition, God wants us to understand that He loves us more than we love ourselves.** He loves us so much that He sent His only Son, Jesus Christ, to live, suffer, shed His blood and die on Calvary's cross for your sin and mine. After Jesus' earth-shaking death that day, He was buried and three days later He rose by the power of God. You remember this verse, don't you? You probably learned it in Sunday School when you were a child: *"For God so loved the world, that He gave His only begotten Son, that whosoever believeth in him should not perish, but have everlasting life"* (John 3:16).

In order to really know God, you must go through His only begotten Son, Jesus Christ. Notice what Jesus Christ said Himself: *"I am the way, the truth, and the life: no man cometh unto the Father, but by me"* (John 14:6).

Jesus Christ is the only way to God. Jesus Christ is the only way to joy, peace and to eternal life. Here is how to accept Him into your heart according to the scriptures: *"That if thou shalt confess with thy mouth the Lord Jesus, and shalt believe in thine heart that God hath raised him from the dead, thou shalt be saved"* (Romans 10:9).

"For whosoever shall call upon the name of the Lord shall be saved" (Romans 10:13).

If you are willing to trust Christ as your Saviour, please pray with me the following prayer: *Heavenly Father, I realize that I am a sinner. For Jesus Christ sake, please forgive me of my sins. I now believe with all of my heart that Jesus Christ died, was buried, and rose again. Lord Jesus, please come into my heart and save my soul and change my life. Amen.*

Dear friend of mine, if you want to know God, the source of all love, joy, peace, real happiness and true success, believe in your heart that Jesus Christ died, was buried and rose for you, and ask Him to come into your heart and save you. And He will. You have God's Word on it.

Beginning with the End in Mind,

Daniel

P.T.:

■ You cannot decide when or where you will die, but you can decide how you will live.

—Selected

■ For the Christian, death is not gloom but glory.

—Selected

150

FAREWELL UNTIL NEXT TIME

Dear Y.B.M.:

I trust that you have enjoyed reading these letters of encouragement and challenge as much as I have enjoyed writing them.

When my little brother got married some years ago, I shared some things with him for his consideration regarding the married life, etc., as all older brothers do, I am sure. After I finished, I quickly told him, using his nickname that his college mates gave him, and told him, "Now, don't try to use the things I'm telling you the same way I am using them. You have to put your 'Tonio' on it." By this I meant, due to the fact that even though we are brothers, we are still two different people, our wives are two different women—my wife was born and raised in Jamaica, your wife was born and raised in America, so you can't just take what I say and just run with it verbatim, you have to put your "Tonio" on it. In other words, you got to "eat the chicken and leave the bones", and apply things or not apply things in a way that is good for you and your wife.

Y.B.M., put your "Tonio" on all that I have shared with you in this book, and in *Letters to Young Black Men* as well.

As we look forward to my next and final book in this trilogy of letters to you entitled, *Even Mo' Letters to Young Black Men,* we will discuss the following important topics:

1. Character
2. Leadership
3. Finances & Business
   And a whole lot more.

Until then, Pray! Think! Do!

Daniel

DISCLAIMER ON QUOTATIONS

Simply because we included a certain quotation in this book, does not necessarily mean that we condone the lifestyle or belief system of the person quoted. We included quotations in this book totally based upon the actual meaning of the words of the quotation and its connection to a particular chapter and not upon the person who said it or wrote it.

How To Obtain More Copies Of *Letters to Young Black Men* or *Mo' Letters To Young Black Men*

Our prayer and desire is to see a copy of this book in the hands of every young black man in America and around the world. You can assist in this great mission.

You can obtain more copies of this book in fine bookstores and other retail outlets across the United States of America.

OR

You may order extra copies via one of the websites listed below:

1. www.TorchLegacy.com
2. www.Amazon.com
3. www.BarnesandNoble.com
4. www.BAMM.com (Books-A-Million)
5. www.Borders.com
6. www.CBD.com (Christian Book Distributors)
7. www.LushenaBks.com
8. www.BlackCBD.com (Black Christian Book Distributors)

Contact Info:

Also, if you have any questions, comments, or need further encouragement, please feel free to e-mail me at:

DW3@torchlegacy.com

If you want to know more about getting to know your Creator, call:

1-877-TORCHLP

Letters to Young Black Men
Study Guide & Leaders Guide

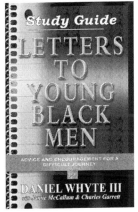
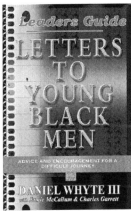

Since the original release of *Letters to Young Black Men*, many have suggested that the book should have a companion study guide so that church leaders, counselors, mentors, and small group leaders could have a resource that would help guide young men through this timely book.

The companion guide for *Letters to Young Black Men* is made up of twenty sessions and is designed for individuals as well as small groups.
- Expounds on the principles laid out in *Letters to Young Black Men*
- Provides questions for discussion
- Gives a summary of each chapter

This study guide for *Letters to Young Black Men* serves as a valuable resource. In it you'll follow the original book, chapter by chapter, and begin to genuinely progress on the success journey. This study guide features over 100 questions adapted from *Letters to Young Black Men* in a format that lets you write your answers directly on to its pages. An answer section allows you to check your work.

Order from: Torch Legacy Publications
www.TorchLegacy.com / 1-877-TORCHLP